UNTIL NOW:
NEW POEMS

By Carrie Newcomer

Available Light Publishing
121 E Kirkwood Ave, Suite 300,
Bloomington, IN 47408
www.carrienewcomer.com

For information about special discounts for bulk purchases, please
contact Available Light Publishing at *contact@mgrfirm.com*

Cover artwork & design by Hugh Syme
Interior design by Tim Gaskins
Edited by Megan Scribner
Back and front cover photo (Carrie the Cyclist) by Jim Krause

The Library of Congress has cataloged this edition as follows Newcomer, Carrie.
Until Now: New Poems / Carrie Newcomer

pages cm
ISBN 978-7375335-0-4

Also by Carrie Newcomer

Books

Music

For more information or to purchase Carrie's books and recordings,
visit www.carrienewcomer.com.

Dedicated to:

Medical professionals, teachers, grocery clerks and all the other essential workers and first responders during the COVID-19 global pandemic.

Table of Contents

NEW POEMS

I'm Learning To Sit With Not Knowing

I'm learning to sit with not knowing.
Even when my restless mind begins jumping
From a worried
What next?
To a frightened
What if?
To a hard edged and impatient,
Why aren't you already there?

I'm learning to sit and listen
To pat myself on the knee,
Lay my hand on my heart,
Take a deep breath,
And laugh at myself.
To befriend my mistakes,
Especially the ones,
That show me how
I most need to change.

I'm learning to sit with whatever comes
(Even though I'm a planner.)
Because so much of this life
Can't be measured or predicted.
Because wonder and suffering visit

When we least expect
And rarely in equal measure.

I'm learning to sit with
What I might never know
Might never learn,
Might never heal.

I'm learning to sit with
What might waltz in and surprise me,
Might crash into my days,
With unspeakable sorrow
Or uncontainable delight.

I'm learning to sit with not knowing.

The Point Of Arrival

At first it felt like a bitter pill,
A rubber band stretched until it snapped.
Sitting cross-legged on the floor
Looking at my empty hands,
Wondering what would become of me,
Now that there was nothing else
But surrender.

First we fold in,
And then we open out.
Acceptance is a kind of ending
And yet, a point of arrival.

This is where I lay down
What can no longer be carried.
This is when I see my hands
Which at first felt so empty
Are filled with
Hallelujah.

Note To Self When Walking

When walking in the woods,
Or on a path,
Or down the street,
Or in a store,
Or just upstairs,
When you are intent on going,
Wherever it is you are going,
Stop.
Stand still.

Notice how your mind can chatter,
Like purple finches in the trees,
Endlessly clicking and warbling,
Rising and falling and rising again.
Notice all your plans and longings,
All the things you got, but didn't want,
All you wanted and didn't get.
Notice all the losses you are carrying,
With as much grace as you can muster.

Notice the sky, the feel of the air on your skin,
The hard knot in your throat,
The sounds, or what hangs in the silence.
Notice all these things and more,

Because there is always more.

Then let your heart crack,
Even just a bit.
A dribble or a dam break,
It doesn't matter.
Because in that opening
You'll discover a clear space.
The one you keep finding,
And losing,
And finding again.

Remember to love it all.
All of it.
Hold hands and high five
With what's easy and dear,
Ephemeral and brilliantly ordinary.
Wrap compassion like a blanket,
The kind we place tenderly,
Around other people's shoulders
When the storm is done and the worst is over.

Love it all,
Without looking for any way out,
Not condoning, just allowing,
For it all to just live,

Where it lives.

Love everything that broke your heart open.

That changed you forever,

That made you softer,

And helped you understand,

What you could not have understood otherwise.

Love what you've endured,

Love what you are still enduring.

Love the purple finches and the sidewalk,

The view from the upstairs window,

The brambles and wild asters,

And the click of the keyboard.

Love all of this

Small and fragile,

Big and beautiful,

Life.

Then,

Take the next step.

The Lake Breathes In.
The Lake Breathes Out.

(for Parker on his birthday)

Ankle deep,

In another high tide,

A silky sheet of water

Pulls itself up and over

The wide, sleeping shoulders of the shore.

The lake breathes in.

The lake breathes out.

I don't know why birthdays are surprising.

I can clearly see up the beach,

The faint overlapping lines in the sand,

The deposits of drift and debris,

Evidence of all that waxes and wanes.

I can even search out and find

A few scattered flood markers

Where storms raked and reformed

The outer surface

And inner landscape.

And yet, every year, when the tide is up

I go down to the water

Where I am quietly comforted
And a little confused
At the sureness of motion
And the restlessness of time.
Feeling the container of my heart fill
With a liquid wonder at my own place
In something so brief
And endless.

The lake breathes in.
The lake breathes out.

Carrying my shoes
Bare feet in the sand.
Let me be here tonight,
In the light of a haloed moon.
Feeling how it pulls seamlessly
At the edges of the sleeping world.
Smiling
At all that is so beautifully
And reverently
Done and undone.

When Things Come Together

I stepped out of my car
With arms full of groceries,
Carrots and potatoes,
Broccoli and onions.
An ordinary sack of ordinary things.

Just then, high overhead,
Came wave upon wave
Of migrating sandhill cranes.
They were elegant and determined,
Calling to one another
Across the clear December sky.

Suddenly,
While I was watching,
A great number released themselves from formation.
They opened and gathered,
Hovered and honked,
Blossoming like spilled ink in blue water,
Skating randomly around like Jesus bugs on a pond.

And then, without any apparent reason
That could be seen from the ground,
They remembered and returned,

Realigned and regained direction.

Catching and attending

To the calling

Of a common commitment

To the pulse of a shared heartbeat

Recreating their connections

Washing forward wing to wing to wing.

Sometimes things come together.

And we don't know why.

Maybe the wind shifted

Or the light changed.

Maybe it was a bit of courage

Or a moment of clarity.

Maybe the eternal called

Or an internal clock chimed.

All I know is that somewhere,

Something keeps weaving.

Creating whole cloth

From what seems hopelessly unraveled.

Something keeps nudging our hearts

In the right general direction,

Pulling the threads

Of membership

Of kinship

Of connection

Mending the gaps

Wing to wing to wing.

Mrs. O'Donohue

I held out my story,
A shy offering
Written with blue crayon,
On four pages of folded notebook paper.
My second-grade teacher, Mrs. O'Donohue,
Wearing sensible shoes and a blue cardigan sweater,
Smiled and said, "Honey, this is a lovely book."
Lovely.

She'd seen through my rudimentary sentences
And disregarded the misspellings.
She skipped over the bent edges and the smudge on the last page.
She did what a true reader and good listener will do.
She dove right down into the deep water of the story
And swam around with her eyes wide open.
She praised my illustrations and asked me questions
And encouraged me to bring her more.
Which I did,
Until there was a stack of my writing
Displayed on the corner of her wooden desk.

There is a knowing that comes with living a story.
There is redemption in sharing a story
Particularly when in the telling

The narrative becomes less mine
And more ours.
But there is an equal potential
In how we choose to hear it.
Hold it,
Consider it.
How we look past the rough edges,
And listen for the heartbeat at the center of the tale.

I am grateful for Mrs. O' Donohue with her shiny, cat-eye glasses.
Thankful that she would stand at the front of the class each morning
And read aloud from chapter books.
Stories about a brave young girl on the prairie
And snowy evenings on a road less traveled.

I am grateful that she taught me how to form a letter.
But more than that,
She taught me how to shape a thought.
I'm thankful for how she showed me
The unadorned art of listening,
Reading down and through to the meaning.
How to hold a story
in my heart
And give it away with gladness.

Parenting

When I look at the old photographs,
The combed back hair and Donna Reed dresses,
I see their steady eyes looking
From a world that no longer exists
To a world they could not imagine.

They were so impossibly young.
Just barely beyond
Their high school yearbook photos.
The requisite sweater with pearls
The buttoned-down shirt.
They were just this side
Of a first job as a typist
And a tour of duty
In a war no one discussed.

I didn't know it then.
Like all children,
I thought they knew what they were doing.
It wasn't until later,
When I became a parent myself,
That I discovered the truth
That we are all pretty much
Making it up as we go.

No instruction manual,

No final authority,

Nothing but the fierceness of love

And the sincerity of our best intentions.

Albeit some of us do better than others.

Some fail completely,

Leaving the shadows of old wounds

That only the wounded can heal.

Because try as we might,

Vowing to do better than we got

Or didn't get,

Even the most loving parents

Make utterly

Catastrophic

Mistakes.

But we do the best we can.

We struggle with decisions.

React in ways that surprise us.

Marvel at how quickly,

How headlong and unstoppable

It all happens.

And now,

We wrestle with sleep

Finally forgiving ourselves

For what we,

What they,

Didn't know at the time.

They were so impossibly,

Impossibly

Young.

Woofing At The World

Occasionally,
For no reason I can discern,
My dog Ella will go into high alert.
She'll stand on the dock down by the pond
Or lean out into the woods behind our house
Or perch like the Lion King on the edge of our garage roof
(set into a hill so no need for a ladder)
and bark.

Bark deep and low
Resonantly and with gravitas,
Echoing off the hills and surrounding ridge tops.
She senses something is coming
Another dog,
A rangey coyote,
Or a drop in the barometric pressure
Signaling a storm is on the way.

Woofing at the World.
As if to say,
"I am here and I see you coming."
"I am awake."
"I am fierce with love."
"You will not come over that hill
Undeterred."

These are days when we must

Lift our noses to the wind,

Incline an ear and read the signs,

Paying close attention to shifts

In tempo or temperature.

It is time to call a truth a truth

A lie a lie.

To say, "I see the tear gas and unmarked cars."

"I am awake."

"I am fierce with love."

And

"You will not come over that hill

Undeterred."

A Million-Mile Tail

(For the Comet Neowise - discovered on March 27, 2020 - and for all the shining comets as they sail out of view.)

There is a comet that passes this way
Every six thousand years or so,
For the briefest
Handful of days.
This week that comet returned,
Coming into view
After ages of absence.

The comet is actually quite small.
A mere acre or two of ice and rock
And yet blooming behind it
Is a million-mile tail.
A smear of diamonds and dust
Curling in its wake.

Some people are like that,
Passing briefly into our orbit
Having no idea of the wide wash of color,
The glittering ash,
They've left expanding behind them.
Tossed like roses
Or kisses into the wind.

And so tonight,

I lift up on my toes

To catch the last glimpse

Of something real,

But rare,

As it slips beyond the horizon,

Heading back home

To the place it began.

The night sparkling with stars

As it swings out of view.

Sing

Songs were never meant to be left
To "the professionals."
Never mind the person who long ago shamed you
Or the church choir member that told you to
Just mouth the words.
Don't worry if your i's are dotted
And your t's are crossed,
Or your pitches are perfectly placed.

Trust me,
If you spend today singing,
If you start by
Humming in the shower,
Then whistling while picking out carrots,
Or singing as you wash dishes,
Or walk in the woods,
Or cross at the traffic light.
You might just begin to feel
Your True Heart
Open.

You might surprise yourself
By doing a little Gene Kelly
Two step and slide

As you sweep into the kitchen,

Or turn up the car radio

As you roll the windows down.

You might remember an old flame

Or catch the first notes of a new idea.

And possibly,

Very possibly.

You will get to the end of the day,

With nothing else to add

Beyond

"Amen."

Making Sense

Finding what makes sense
In senseless times
Takes grounding myself
Sometimes quite literally,
In the ancient patterns
Of the living world,
Water and stone, animal and tree.
In the layers of soil
Faithfully recreating itself
Year after year,
Leaf atop leaf.

It takes steadying myself
Upon shale and clay and solid rock
Swearing allegiance to an ageless aquifer
Betting on all the still hidden springs.

When so much is unsure
I can believe in a tree.
Trust its broad-leafed perspective,
Dedicated to breathing in, and then out,
Reaching down and then up.

When so much feels without reason

I reach out for a strong trunk

Where I can lay my hands

Or rest my back

And abide for a while between

Its splayed and mossy feet.

I can trust a tree's careful

And drawn out

Way of speaking

     One thoughtful sentence

          Covering the span of many seasons.

A tree doesn't hurry.

A tree doesn't lie.

It knows how to stand true to itself.

Unselfconscious of its beauty and scars,

All the physical signs of where and when

It needed to bend

Rather than break.

A tree stands alone and yet in deepest communion.

For in the gathering of the many,

There is comfort and courage,

Perseverance and protection,

From the storms that howl down from predictable

Or unexplainable directions.

In a senseless time

I hold close to what never stopped

Making sense.

Like love

Like trees

Like how a seed becomes a sapling,

And a sapling becomes a canopy of branches.

Like the scent at the very top of an infant's head

Because there is nothing more right than that.

Nothing.

It is all still happening.

Even now.

Even now.

Liminality

So much of what we know
Lives just below the surface.
Half of a tree
Spreads out beneath our feet.
Living simultaneously in two worlds,
Each half informing and nurturing
The whole.
A tree is either and neither
But mostly both.

I am drawn to liminal spaces,
The half-tamed and unruly patch
Where the forest gives way
And my little garden begins.
Where water, air, and light overlap
Becoming mist on the morning pond.

I like to sit on my porch steps, barn jacket and boots
In the last long exhale of the day,
When bats and birds loop in and then out,
One rising to work,
One readying for sleep.

And although the full moon calls the currents,
And the dark moon reminds me

That my best language
Has always emerged out of the silence,
It is in the waxing and waning
Where I most often live,
Neither here nor there,
But simply
On the way.

There are endings and beginnings
One emerging out of the other.
But most days I travel in an ever present
And curious now.
A betwixt and between,
That is almost,
But not quite,
The beautiful,
But not yet.

I've been learning to live with what is,
More patient with the process,
To love what is becoming,
And the questions that keep returning.

I am learning to trust
The horizon I walk toward
Is an orientation,
Not a destination.

And that I will keep catching glimpses

Of something great and luminous

From the corner of my eye.

I am learning to live where loss holds fast

And where grief lets loose and unravels.

Where a new kind of knowing can pick up the thread.

Where I can slide palms with a paradox

And nod at the dawn,

As the shadows pull back

And spirit meets bone.

What You Won't Hear On Cable News

I want to tell you
What you won't hear on cable news.
About a young woman in the airport
Who was so exhausted and harried
By hours of delay
And wrangling an overtired toddler
That when her little boy
Finally and completely
Melted down
And planted himself on the floor,
She sat down beside him
And started to cry.

I want to tell you about five random women
Who immediately flowed in from all directions.
One pulled out a little toy from her purse,
One offered a snack or to go get something to drink,
One who called the child "Honey"
Wiped his nose with a tissue
And offered another one to the grateful mother.
And the one who asked if it was alright
To walk hand in hand with the child
Right there at the gate,
Close by and always, always in sight.

I want to tell you about a man

Who makes soup and bread

And then gives it away.

And the nurse who held his hand

When he was breathless and afraid.

I want to tell you about my neighbor

Who drives around all winter

With snow chains in his car

Just in case someone needs help.

I want to tell you about all the people I meet

Who keep extending themselves,

And braving the risk

Of being told

It's none of their business.

Who offer a hand,

Or a bit of encouragement,

Or a couple of bucks.

Who will walk a fussy child around the gate.

Because it is the kind thing to do.

I want to tell you the world still turns

Every single day

On an axis of goodness

And unexpected grace

That shows up without fanfare

And often where we least expect to find it.

Turning The Soil

He came to do some yardwork.
Hired to mulch and weed while I was away.
When I returned
I discovered that this earnest young man
Had mistaken the herbs and perennial flowers
For weeds.
And then neatly and efficiently
Removed whole beds of growth,
Leaving only the weeds,
(which in his defense also had blooms)
Unharmed and undisturbed.

For days, I avoided going outside.
Every time I'd look, I could only see
What was no longer there.
Years of carefully tended plants
French lavender, English thyme, chives, oregano
Hyssop, marjoram, borage, three kinds of mint,
Beds of Veronica, bee balm, Russian blue sage,
Were all gone.
Gone.

Like her
Like my beautiful, bawdy, graceful friend

Who had recently surrendered
To an invasive cancer, a creeping illness
That no one could pull out, prune back
Or stop from advancing until it finally overran,
Her brave and embattled body.
She was gone.

Finally, days later,
I put on my gloves, gathered my tools,
And began pulling the weeds.
I pruned and clipped, shoveled and hoed.
I hacked back and reclaimed
Piling up the brush and trimmings,
The creeping Charlie and thorny brambles,
And finally hauled it all out into the woods.

Then, after hours of angry, grief-stricken work,
I lay down on my back
Sank into that barren mulched landscape
There beside where my garden had been,
And wept like a child.

I wailed into the empty sky,
Letting the tears roll down my face,
I wept for my lost garden.
I wept for my lost friend.

I wept for how often people
And death,
So carelessly stomp around
In what takes years to love and nurture,
And randomly take
What cannot be replaced.

After a long time
I got back up, wiped my eyes,
Picked up my shovel,
And began preparing the ground.
I couldn't change what's been lost.
But eventually
Something is going to grow
In that ravaged ground.

I can choose whether that will be
Weeds of bitterness
A limiting grief
Or something that may someday
Expand the heart
And bloom with purpose.

But not now.
Perhaps not for a very long time.

I returned to my planting,

Knowing that what has been lost

Is never completely gone.

Knowing that the moon will go dark,

Before it begins inching back.

Knowing that an uprooted garden mends slowly.

And that the broken earth

And broken hearts

Can be healed.

When the brush has been cleared

And the soil has been turned

And the rain finally comes.

Send Love. It Matters.

Somewhere someone needs help.
Send love.
It matters.

If you can't get there yourself,
Then take a deep breath.
Breathe in the weight of their troubles.
Breathe out and send all those burdens
Into the Light
Where sorrows can be held
With the most tender and infinite grace.

Breathe in what you can do.
Breathe out what you can't change.
Spool out a thread of connection,
Send courage and calm.
For the nights can be long
And filled with shadows,
And sometimes terrible
Unexpected waters will rise.

Somewhere someone needs help.
Send love.
It matters.

Egg Gourds

In my exuberance and anticipation
I plant too many,
And then,
Do not have the heart,
To thin out the small ones.
I mean, doesn't every shoot
Have a right to a little sun?
Deserve a chance
To elbow into the world?
Which I admit is my gardener's Achilles heel,
And why my radishes will always be abundant but small.

So the gourds, they all grew
Flourishing with wild green abandon
Covering the raised beds and climbing up
And then over
The garage roof.
They unfurled yellow blossoms
Which became small green nobs,
Which grew into hanging gourds,
That looked exactly,
Precisely,
Like white chicken eggs.

At that point I should have pulled out a few,
Pinched them back,
Reined them in.
I mean they were crowding out the rhubarb
And replacing the dill.

But all I could do
Was watch in wonder.
Admire and applaud
How these earnest plants,
With apparently no practical purpose
Beyond being ample
And amusing
And audacious,
Could be so gloriously themselves.
Completely content to be nothing more
Or less
Than simply
And utterly
Delightful.

Even Then

Twilight on the ridge top,
I came upon two lanky coyotes
And one large coydog.
They all wore thick grey wolf-like coats
And a hungry look.
Lily, my 48-pound herding dog mix,
Sped into the woods barking.
Doing what her deep down DNA demanded -
Keep the herd safe,
Whatever it takes.

The three wild canines ran off a little way,
But quickly returned when they realized
The relative size of my small guardian angel.
I saw them begin to circle her as a team.
I heard her yelp high and distressed.
I ran crashing through the brush,
Brambles catching my pant legs and jacket edges,
Whistling long shrill notes between my fingers,
A trick I'd learned when I was eight years old.
(Who knows when we might need a gift from our former self?)

The coyotes looked up,
Surprised.

The largest one met my eyes, assessing me.

Predators don't expect prey to have friends in the world

Who are willing to run headlong into danger,

Sound an alarm,

And shout with righteous anger.

The pack of three looked at one another,

Shrugged and then half loped, half glided

Off into the darkening woods.

Lily was unhurt but concerned and trembling.

I held her collar securely,

Knowing she was absolutely ready to go after the pack,

If I should only ask.

I ruffled her ears,

Me the small and she the somewhat smaller,

And wondered at the enormous size and courage

Of a small dog's heart

And was grateful to know

That she had me covered.

And that I had her back.

And love does prevail,

Even in the twilight

Even when the coyotes circle.

Yes, even then.

Redeemable

Happy Leap Year!

Happy Intercalary Day!

The day when we gather up

The uncounted or misplaced

Extra minutes and hours.

The day when we fish out

All the seconds of spare change

That somehow ended up

Between the couch cushions of time.

The day we roll them all up,

Trade in the whole lot

For a new and shiny silver dollar day.

Imagine that.

The possibility of gathering up

The small and fleeting things we missed.

Using some mysterious alchemy

That combines lost and found

Into a new insight.

A humble but surprising

Leap of understanding

About what slips out of our pockets

If we're not paying attention.

Meeting Myself

Once I met myself at the corner of State Street and Main.
She didn't notice me.
I had arrived from the unseeable future
And she was a resident of the unchangeable past.
She was pulling on the handle of a children's wagon,
With its red paint and one wobbly wheel,
Bouncing and rattling over every sidewalk crack.

I've met myself other times,
Whisps of myself that show up
During visits to haunted places
Or in daydreams
Or memories that wash over
For no reason at all.
Once in a grocery line
With a baby on my hip
Rocking and shifting
The way that mothers have always done.
Humming in the way that mothers always do.
Once on the shores of Lake Michigan
Coming up out of the water,
A preacher's hand on my head
Singing *There Is A Balm In Gilead.*

Once when I was driving my car at 3am

The hour when only drunks

And musicians

Are trying to get home.

And once in an apartment that was too cold,

And a relationship that burned too hot.

And then that time when an elderly woman at the ice cream stand

Looked down at my billowing maternity sundress

And gave me an extra scoop.

I met myself on that terrible day

When I lost what had been so intimately attached,

Like Peter Pan's shadow

Sewn on to his feet by Wendy's quick needle.

Once in my mother's kitchen

And again, in a therapist office.

Once at the top of a mountain

Pouring out a container of ash.

It seems as I get older

The more glimpses I get.

So often unbidden,

Memories I savor, still puzzle, and grieve.

And so here I am,

Right now, at the keyboard

Writing about ghosts

Sensing perhaps

At this very moment

Just over my shoulder

I might already be standing,

Remembering this intersection

Of my life and these words.

Pretending

I pretended it was alright.

Because I wanted it to be alright.

If I could just dim the lights,

Drape a t-shirt over

The too bright hotel lamp

Of all that was unspoken.

If I stuck to the script,

Stayed in the center,

Avoided the dangerous edges,

I would be safe.

I could go on

Not knowing

What I already knew.

But eventually,

If we are lucky,

Our hearts break.

Or the t-shirt catches fire,

Or we get very quiet.

Or we are loved for exactly who we are.

And finally, the circumstances press the point

Until we find a new language

And create a new frame.
Let go of being ashamed
Or practical or sensible.
And finally stop pretending,
It's alright when it's not.

Let the lamp light up the room,
Showing the shape of a door,
And open it.

Into Every Conversation

Into every conversation,
At least those that matter,
I carry my stories like a book
Tucked under my arm or secured
Deep in my heart.
A foreword written by the ancestors,
Side notes and commentary in the margins,
Written by mentors, tormentors, and friends.

I bring my grief and my losses.
When hopes melted like salt in the rain.
When a beloved passed from this world
And the world went on.

I bring the longings of my Italian great-grandfather
Who was caught tacking up a thesis on the local church door.
His penance to lick the aisle of the church from door to altar.
The same man who reached the altar,
Spat the blood in his mouth at the priest,
Packed up his family and moved to Chicago
— and never licked a floor again.

Every one of us, brings the horizons never reached by our ancestors
And the port of entry experienced by the ones who did.

We bring brutalities and resilience,

Old disappointments and new babies.

We bring memories of kindnesses and acts of aggression.

We bring all we know and still don't know.

I bring my ignorance and othering.

Privileges I couldn't or didn't acknowledge.

Until I did.

Believing that the color of my hands

(That now look so much like my grandmother's)

Was normative.

Until it wasn't.

I bring what is passionate and humbling,

And a determination to take the mud from my eyes

And do the next right thing.

There are those who would say,

Don't bring history into this conversation,

I wasn't there, so what does it matter now?

Don't bring what you know and live each and every day.

Don't bring the stories you learned

As a matter of survival.

Don't bring your mother or father,

Your sister or brother, son or daughter.

Don't bring all you've encountered,
Transcendent or down close to the bone.

And yet, into every conversation,
At least those that matter,
We bring it all.
Must bring it all.
Welcome it all.
Particularly the hard parts,
Especially the human and loving parts,
And always the parts that dare
And dare again to hope
And keep on hoping.

I began this poem after a conversation with Dr. Luther E. Smith, Jr. and Parker J. Palmer for The Growing Edge Podcast. At one point, Smith spoke about the stories we carry, our own stories, and the stories of those who came before us. I was so moved by his words, particularly when he said, "Don't ask me to enter into a conversation without the whole of my experience and history," which prompted this poem.

Revolution, The Day After

Revolution is finding your horizon
And then walking toward it.
Knowing that you will be walking
      For a very long while,
            Or always.
Because the process of getting there,
Because bringing in a better world,
Will take more than your one lifetime.

Revolution is traveling light,
Leaving what's dead weight
By the side of the road.
      Like vengeance
            And stone-cold hatred
That expands and gets heavier,
Like slow-drying cement,
In the chambers of your heart.

Revolution is holding close
All you love,
All you believe in,
All you hope for.
Everything that actually matters.

Because you're going to get tired

    and discouraged

        and angry

            and wander off course.

You're going to need
What you've gathered,
Embraced and endured.
Because it's love,
Always love,
That will tug on your sleeve
And remind you to look up,

    Search the sky for True North.

        Get a bead on something

          Improbable

            Shining and unstoppable

        And keep walking.

Not Even Close

It's a hard day, but not the only day.

Because even now

When justice was not served

We gathered in and gathered up what we love.

Like one another

Like our dogs and our kids

Like the way the ground smells after it rains

Like the silence after the last note of a beautiful song

Like a newly discovered spring of unexpected laughter

Like the poem or the book or the image that changed everything

Like lighting bugs and a gibbous moon.

Like the memories we will take to our last days saying,

"Yes, oh yes, now that was fine."

Like babies doing that bouncing baby dance they do

Like tender green buds after a long hard winter

Like the way that water eddies around stones in the river

Like a good apple and homemade soup,

Clean sheets and a warm sweater.

Like the birds that gather in murmuring flocks,

Like the hills and valleys of this place,

That were here before we arrived into this world,

And will be here long after we are gone.

Like the patterns of tree limbs and roots

Which look like the branches of our lungs,

Like the rivers and streams

Reaching out from the coastline into the heart of the land.

Like the elegant way a butterfly opens and closes itself

Like the round little wooly worm, nibbling leaves and dreaming of wings

Like the seasons, one following another,

Each filled to overflowing with purpose.

Like how far we've come,

And what is honorable about the work yet to do.

Like the light on the morning pond

And the glow in the evening sky.

Like the ache of longing and of the joy of returning

Like the hand as it lays upon ours

Saying, "All will be well."

All these things, and so much more,

Everything beautiful and unbroken,

Life giving and life sustaining,

Are not out there somewhere.

But all right here,

Within us

And between us.

It is a hard day.

But not the only day.

Not even close.

Forest Bathing

Two phoebes whistle across the hollow.
Newly open leaves excitedly whisper,
Rustling like young women in their first formal dresses.
Creek water slides softly over grey and brown stones.
The shadow of a hawk, ripples over the ground,
A chipmunk dives beneath a rotted log.

Everything is in motion,
The new ferns,
The wild bee balm,
The clutch of salamander eggs, soon to hatch,
The beech and sycamore, shagbark hickory and oak,
Even the stones, wearing down,
Year by year.

I stop on the trail
And close my eyes.
I begin to imagine I am growing my own roots.
My soul reaching down
Into the loam
1 inch
   6 inches,
      1 foot,
         1 yard,

                6 feet then

                        12 feet

                                down,

There in the dark,

I introduce myself to all that is alive.

Listening for what just might want to

Introduce itself to me.

Then after a long while, and with a touch of regret,

I call up my soul and bring back my roots,

To return

To a place where I'm only

Touching the ground

Through my shoes.

But when I walk on,

I am now quietly breathing

Noticing how

The leaf-filtered light

Feels like a kiss

And every step

Is taken

Ever so

Reverently.

A Sign

Sunday afternoon,
An off-clinic outing,
A group of bulimic and anorexic women
Painting pottery,
They are talking about how to get better,
But not too much better,
At least not too fast,
Because insurance you know.
Tips and tricks for how to progress
Slightly
Because they'll also cut you off
If they think you're not trying.
And this kind of healing
Takes courage,
And determination,
And especially time.

The group was comprised
Of mostly middle-aged and multi-racial women.
Not one stereotype at the table.
Each and every one of them
Carrying ragged-edged membership cards
To a fellowship no one wanted to join,
And trying very hard
Not to die.

While the two well-dressed women
Painting Christmas ornaments at the next table
Lean in,
Just barely,
Listening,
In the same way that people
Drive by highway accidents
Glancing with raw curiosity
At the shape of the wreckage
The twisted metal and lights flashing.
Unable to look away.

Then I noticed
On the wall
Just above the group
Hangs a brightly painted platter
Beaming out the bold words,
"You're So Pretty."
The irony was deafening.
The black humor breathtaking.

But then I think
Perhaps
Just maybe
This is not some random existential joke.
But rather

An affirmation.

A wink from the future.

A sign from the god

Of damaged

And finally mended things.

Luminous

(This poem was the seed that began the song "On The Day You Were Born.")

On the day you were born,
Something shining came with you.
Something that was already you,
And only you,
Arrived.

On the day you were born,
The world opened up
And welcomed you
Into the turning of seasons,
The phases of the moon,
The migration of birds,
The in and out breathing
Of the tides.

On the day you were born,
The wind held true to its course,
The creeks rose and fell,
And the trees reached down and then up.

On the day you were born,
Fire burned in the West
And snow fell in the North.

The clock didn't stop
You just stepped into time.

On the day you were born,
I was forever assured
Yet forever uncertain,
How it happens and what it is
That comes and then leaves,
Is sent and recalled,
From luminous to luminous.
To live for a while
In all that is luminous in between.

On the day you were born,
Something shining came with you,
Something that was already you,
And only you,
Arrived.

When I Most Want To Rush

When I most want to rush
Perhaps,
It is time to slow down.

What might happen,
If I stopped trying to get to the epilogue,
Before I read the middle chapters?

Maybe I would breathe into
Right where I am
And love what I find there.
Know that wherever I am
Is right where I need to be,
And lose all interest
In runaway trains.

I can keep drinking from a firehose
That drenches me
Without quenching my thirst.
Or I can taste one drop of honey
Let it rest on my tongue
Until it is gone.

I'm not saying that I should give up.

Or stop.
But just begin to live this,
And then that.
Breathing into one true thing,
And then into the next.

And finally learn,
When I most want to rush
It is time to slow down.

Bearing Witness

The trees on this hill are luminous.
A collective of spring green leaves
That seem to glow
From within.
Amid the new foliage
Dark branches are still visible
In patches and places,
Dramatic as inked lines on a page.

They are gathered together
Like a circle of women.
Some young and slender.
Some with babies on their hips.
Some barely standing, bent over with age.
And now having seen
Their way through another long winter,
Let their leaves open and unfurl
Like untying their hair.

Nothing lasts forever,
Not even winter.
This is the way the forest bears witness
To all that is soft and heavy,
Lost and lasting,

Pardoned and persisting,
How beginnings usually come
When something else ends.

And each year, the wood thrush
and lighting bugs come back
Winking off
And then on.
A mystic
      Morse
            Code.

The Shape Of A Heart

The beech trees on this ridge are old companions.
Trunks like sturdy elephant legs
Smooth and grey.
Willowy when young,
Straight and stately as they age.

I lay my hands on one of the trees
Flat palmed like a Baptist blessing,
Putting my ear to the bark
Listening for her pulse.

There is a charred hole about thirty feet up.
Evidence of a long-ago storm
A crash of thunder,
A lightning strike,
A natural event,
A blameless bit of bad luck.

It is a wonder she survived,
Living with and then into
Her most devastating wound.
Sending out new branches
To counterbalance and protect
What had been weakened.

Until now

After years of patient mending

The gash has mostly grown over.

Creating something singular

Unexpected and unlikely,

Even beautiful.

Because what was broken

Has been healed

Leaving an opening

In the miraculous

Shape of a heart

And what of myself

When lightning strikes,

When the smoke scatters,

And stress points are made clear?

Will I be able

To shore up what needs mending

And shift my old concepts

Of what it means to be whole?

To inch by inch, love my way into

A new version of being healed.

Not lacking,

Just different,

And still utterly true.

As that unexpected

And miraculous

Shape of a heart

I Don't Know Why

I don't know why
We get so lost
And afraid
And misguided
And mistaken.

Why we fall down in sludgy heaps of resentment
Or hate
And then stay there.
Maybe because it's familiar.
Maybe because it doesn't require much.
Maybe because this version of violence
Feels justified.
Sanctified.

All I know is that we do.

I don't know why - or even how
We continue to rise up.
Then stand up.

Choosing (because it is always a choice)
To be kind
Or brave
Or funny and true.

Or find the grace to listen,
And the courage to speak.

I don't know how we keep imagining
What could and should be,
When we are still right in the middle of
What is.
I don't know how we breathe again,
Start again
And remember to look up,
Checking if our feet are aligned
With the most faithful star.

I don't know how we keep pouring out
All the beauty we can create,
Cup after cup
Into the waiting basin of the world,
So that we might wash off the mud
Before it's too deep.

I don't know why we can stray
So utterly far
And yet,
Again and again,
Find our way back,
To what is utterly true.

I don't know why
Or how.
All I know is, we do.

Acknowledgements

Armloads of gratitude to my editor, Megan Scribner. It was the greatest pleasure to collaborate with you in the writing and editing of this book of poetry. Your insights, suggestions, and how you thoughtfully approached these poems from their spiritual center and my best intentions made all the difference.

Thank you to my husband, Robert, who has always believed in me and in my writing. Thank you for your support and endless enthusiasm, for your ability to imagine new ideas and bring them life. Many of these poems were written during the COVID-19 pandemic, a year of great unraveling. Thank you for being a true companion and awesome euchre partner.

Deepest gratitude to Parker J. Palmer, my dear friend and treasured mentor. Many of these poems were sent to you before anyone else saw them. Thank you for the conversations and letters, insights, comments, and encouragement. My life is richer because you are in it.

Appreciation to Gary Walters for the gift of our collaborations over these many years. My life and art are deeper and truer because of our time together, personally and musically.

Thank you to Amelia, my friends, and family. The women of Meadowlark Farm, Anam Cara, and the Fab Five.

Thank you to Tim, Kelly, Hugh, Kayla, and Kappy. Your amazing talents and time were instrumental in the creation of this book.

About the Author

Carrie Newcomer is a songwriter, recording artist, performer, educator, and activist. She has been described as a "prairie mystic" by the Boston Globe and one who "asks all the right questions" by Rolling Stone Magazine. Carrie has 19 nationally released albums on Available Light & Concord/Rounder Records including *Until Now, The Point Of Arrival,* and *The Beautiful Not Yet.* She also has three books of poetry and essays. Her song "I Should've Known Better" appeared on Nickel Creeks' Grammy-Winning gold album, *This Side,* and she earned an Emmy for the PBS special, *An Evening With Carrie Newcomer.*

In 2009 and 2011 Newcomer was invited by the American Embassy of India to be a cultural ambassador, resulting in her interfaith benefit album *Everything is Everywhere* with Amjad Ali Khan, the master of the Indian Sarod. She was awarded an honorary degree in Music for Social Change from Goshen College and was the 2019 recipient of The Shalem Institute's Contemplative Voices Award.

In recent years, Carrie joined with beloved author Parker J. Palmer to create *The Growing Edge* collaboration which explores growing edges, personally, vocationally, and politically. Together they create live events, personal growth retreats, and the highly rated *The Growing Edge Podcast.* Spirituality and Health Magazine named Parker and Carrie two of the top ten spiritual leaders for the next twenty years.

Carrie is known for her low and resonant voice "as rich as Godiva Chocolate" according to *The Austin Statesman,* for the depth of her music and the poetry of her lyrics, as well as for the progressive spiritual content of her songs, poetry, and workshops. Carrie lives in the wooded hills of South Central Indiana with her husband and two shaggy rescue dogs.

Made in the USA
Las Vegas, NV
13 January 2023

65570854R00052